10 STEPS TO WALKING NICELY ON A LOOSE LEASH
- Step by Step Instructions to Support Your Training Sessions

Table of Contents

10 STEPS TO WALKING NICELY ON A LOOSE LEASH

- Step by Step Instructions to Support Your Training Sessions

Table of Contents (cont'd)

INTRODUCTION

Do you have a dog that pulls you along like a steam train pulling freight? Do you secretly dread walking your dog because they pull the leash so tight that it makes your arms and shoulders ache? If so, walks are probably miserable for you, and, undoubtedly, for your dog too.

You Aren't Alone!

Many dogs pull when on leash. This doesn't just make walks unpleasant; it can even be dangerous for both you and your dog.
Walking nicely is a life skill that when missing can significantly and negatively impact the human-canine relationship resulting in fewer walks, less exercise, and a decrease in social exposure for the dog.

Let's Change That!

Leash walking issues can be very frustrating for you and for your dog but, with the help of the 10 Steps to Walking Nicely on a Loose Leash E-Workbook, and with safe, humane, and fun training techniques, you will soon be on the road to improving both you and your dog's leash skills.

Helping Dogs Lead Fulfilled & Enriched Lives!

Teaching your dog to walk nicely on a loose leash takes patience and time, but even committing to just ten minutes of daily training will put you both on the path to leash walking success! The time you spend working through this fun program will be well worth it when you're out enjoying a lovely stroll with your best friend!

The training games will not only improve your dog's leash walking skills, leading to a dog that is a pleasure to take out; they will improve your skills too! The result will be more walks, more exercise, more mental and physical enrichment, more social exposure, more fun time spent together, and even an increase in the bond that you share with each other!

DEFINITION OF WALKING NICELY ON A LOOSE LEASH AND OUR GOALS

Our goal when teaching a dog to walk nicely on leash is **NOT** that your dog walks in an 'obedience style heel-position'; rather that your dog is able to walk with you, and that both you and your dog work towards the maintenance of a loose leash.

What we hope that you will achieve by the end of this program:
1. Your dog will learn how to walk nicely on a loose leash without pulling you, the guardian.
2. You will learn how to respond should your dog pull or lunge forwards.
3. You will learn how to walk your dog without tightening the leash. Yes, humans pull too!
4. You will have the tools and the knowledge to continue to practice your skills and to generalize them to different environments.
5. You will improve the relationship that you and your dog share with each other.
6. You will communicate more clearly with your dog.
7. Your dog's focus on you will increase.
8. Your focus on your dog will also increase!
9. You will both enjoy spending time together.
10. You will look forward to your walks!

DEFINITION OF WALKING NICELY ON A LOOSE LEASH AND OUR GOALS

Let's further clarify:

• The initial goal of this program will be that your dog is able to stand on a loose leash.

• This will be followed by your dog being able to move with you, when directly in front of and facing you, for very short distances, in non-distracting environments. This means that you will initially be walking backward!

• The goal that we aim to achieve by the end of this program is that your dog can happily walk near your side for at least 20 dog-lengths. You will not pull your dog and your dog will not pull you. There will be no tension on the leash.

• The final goal, which we are sure you will aim for, is that of successfully removing the strain from both the leash and from your walks, so that you and your dog can enjoy lots of fun outings together! This final goal is one that can be developed in future classes or by following the additional tips for proofing and maintaining your leash walking skills that are included in your 10 Steps to Walking Nicely on a Loose Leash E-Workbook.

Helping Dogs Lead Fulfilled & Enriched Lives

About DogNostics

DogNostics is an affordable, science based, ethical educational provider for pet professionals. DogNostics provides you with a wide range of educational programs from webinars to short learning courses, all the way to multi-level certificate and diploma programs. With DogNostics, you get everything from the art and science of dog training to how to effectively market your business services and increase your income!

YES, We Are Different ...
Being Different is What Sets Us Apart!

First, we are all certified people trainers or teachers and secondly, we are all highly experienced pet business owners and pet professionals with a wide array of experience and credentials. Third, we are passionate about the future of our industry and the development of those who practice within it. Lastly, we all love what we do and helping others to achieve their individual goals. At DogNostics we provide education that is fun and easy to access at affordable rates!

Your DogNostics program can be started as soon as you register and undertaken from the comfort of your own home! You get the support you need through interactive groups, email, telephone and internet meetings in a way that works for you.

YOUR WORKBOOK FORMAT

- Over a course of easy-to-follow lessons, you will master the '10 Steps to Walking Nicely on a Loose Leash'.
- Before sharing the essential skills that you and your dog will learn, we have included ten key pieces of knowledge that will help ensure ongoing success!
- There are also three essential skills to learn before you get started with the '10 Steps to Walking Nicely on a Loose Leash'.
- All the training skills are taught in the order in which you should progress.
- You will also learn fun games and activities that can be used to proof and generalize your newly acquired skills!

There are Many Ways to Train a Behavior 

We have tried to keep this program as achievable as possible for both you, the pet dog guardian, and for your dog. If you are taking classes, your force-free trainer may include more, fewer, or even some different training steps.

Skill Training 'Recipes'

This program is a 'recipe', and like all recipes, the ingredients sometimes need adapting to suit an individual. Many dogs will quickly and successfully progress through the training steps. Some dogs may take longer to achieve some of the steps; and some may even need additional steps – a few extra 'ingredients' for success. We have included lots of suggestions to help you, but please use the Train-Test-Train system to guide you, and, if in doubt, contact your force-free training professional.

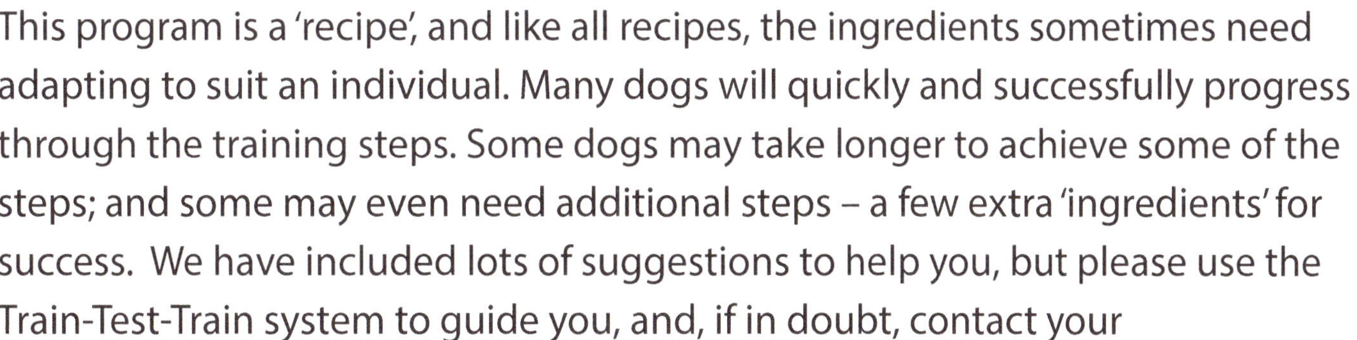

IMPORTANT INFORMATION

There are several important points that we would like to emphasize so that you can integrate them not just into this training program, but also into your daily life with your canine companion.

1. The more you 'mark' and reinforce (reward) the lovely behaviors that you would like your dog to repeat, the more your dog will do them. Positive reinforcement strengthens behaviors!

2. We all need to become "Yes" people! We need to clearly communicate with our dogs when they are doing the right thing! At the exact moment that your dog achieves the desired behavior, you should say "yes" (or click).

3. Behaviors that are reinforced will be repeated! It is crucial to remember that after you mark a behavior, you should immediately feed a tasty treat.

4. When training our dogs, we should use the Train-Test-Train system. Training in sets of five will helps guide you as to whether your dog is struggling slightly and you need to make the training game easier; whether your dog is progressing well but needs a bit more practice at the current step and you, therefore, need to repeat the same level; or whether your dog is ready to move on to the next, slightly more difficult, step.

IMPORTANT INFORMATION
(CONT'D)

5. We need to bear in mind that the most important behaviors that we ask our dogs to carry out, such as walking nicely on a loose leash, and more difficult behaviors, such as walking nicely on a loose leash in the face of distractions, in more challenging environments, need more powerful reinforcement consequences (bigger rewards). If we expect more, and we are teaching more difficult skills, then we must pay accordingly!

6. We need to have shared meaning regarding not only the importance of using high value reinforcement but what high value means. In a home environment, where there are no distractions - nothing more interesting to your dog than you and your training game -, you can probably use your dog's food or, for example, some nutritious shop-bought treats. However, out and about you will need a more 'valuable' reinforcement consequence: one from higher up your dog's Hierarchy of Rewards: Special treats such as sausage, chicken, turkey, beef heart, steak, cheese… Something that your dog loves and does not usually get. We also advise that the treats be slightly moist, as this makes them easy to chew and swallow, and nice and smelly - A dog's nose recognizes the odor of a delicious treat!

7. If you diligently work through all the training games that are included in this program and all the criteria – the different training steps – that are included in each game; use appropriate rewards; only increase the level of difficulty when your dog

IMPORTANT INFORMATION
(CONT'D)

has accomplished the current step; and do not skip any of the training steps even if your dog is progressing well…. Then, by the end of this short course, you and your dog should be well on the road to enjoyable shared walks!

8. The goal of the 10 Steps to Walking Nicely on a Loose Leash is not just that of training nice leash walking skills but also that all the training games should be lots of fun for you both. We do not just wish to improve the skills of pet dog guardians and their dogs; we also want you to increase the bond that you share, while enjoying additional mental and physical enrichment together!

IMPORTANT INFORMATION
Dogs are NOT Machines

Please note that, although via systematic training and lots of positive reinforcement, you will undoubtedly improve both your and your dog's leash walking skills, we cannot and should not ever guarantee that a dog will demonstrate 100% compliance to any cue. This is an unrealistic expectation.

We must remember that behavior is a function of the environment. Dogs are not machines; they are sentient beings who have their own thoughts and emotions. Just like humans, dogs have the ability to make their own decisions, and those decisions might not always align with our desires. Sometimes a dog might not respond to a cue; sometimes there might be a delay in the response.

Perhaps…

- Something in the environment is impacting your dog's ability to respond.
- Your dog does not consider it safe to respond at that particular time.
- Your dog is aware of something that you haven't noticed.

- Your dog didn't hear you.
- There is something very interesting in the environment that requires your dog's immediate attention and/or investigation.
- You haven't trained the behavior as well as you thought.
- You are simply asking too much of your dog in this environment, at this stage in their learning and development.

IMPORTANT INFORMATION

Handling a Dog

Trainers: During the process of teaching a dog to walk nicely on leash, you will be handling the students' dogs more often than in most other situations. Please ensure that all dogs are happy to have their collars/harnesses/leashes held prior to class. We also advise addressing this important topic again in the first class to make sure that everyone understands how important it is that their dogs are happy to be handled.

Guardians: We encourage you to condition a positive emotional response (a happy response) to the holding of your dog's collar, harness, and leash by repeatedly pairing with delicious treats.

If your dog demonstrates any body language signals that might indicate that they are uncomfortable with being handled…

- If you are taking a class, please communicate this to your class trainer/instructor who will be able to advise you.
- If you are training your dog yourself, please contact a knowledgeable force-free dog trainer or behavior consultant.

IMPORTANT INFORMATION

Leash Reactivity

Important! Please note that if you have a problem with leash 'reactivity', you should consult a certified, force-free behavior consultant.

For example,
- Your dog reacts negatively to other dogs or people while being walked on leash.
- Your dog barks, lunges, pulls, snaps, snarls or growls at other dogs or people.
- Your dog shows body language signals indicative of a fearful response.
- Your dog exhibits escape or avoidance behavior.

LEASH WALKING TOOLS FOR SUCCESS!

Although your key tool for success will be your committed relationship built on mutual respect, empathy, trust, and attentiveness, choosing the appropriate equipment will also be instrumental in the process of training your dog to walk nicely on leash, while ensuring their emotional and physical well-being, and the successful completion of this program.

Recommended

1. A well-fitting, non-restrictive harness.

• For larger dogs and those dogs that tend to pull, we recommend a harness that has both front and back rings as, if needed, the leash can be attached at both points. Alternatively, a front-ring only harness is a good choice. Using the front attachment will assist you while you and your dog are working on your leash walking skills as, if your dog pulls towards something, the front leash attachment point will cause them to pivot their chest toward you. *Please note that some harnesses, although they have a front ring, have not been manufactured with the intention of this being the sole ring used.
• For smaller dogs and those dogs who are just getting started with walking nicely on leash, who have no prior history of pulling or being pulled, a back ring harness may be suitable.

2. A nylon or leather 2m / 6ft leash. 

We love multi-positional leashes – also referred to as training leashes, multi-functional leashes, or police dog leashes. These are leashes that have a trigger hook at each end and O-rings placed at intervals along the leash. The length of the leash can, therefore, be adjusted when needed. They are also a good option for those who wish to walk 'hands-free'.

3. A treat bag full of tasty treats.

Treat bags with an adjustable waist belt will mean that your treats are easily accessible and that you do not need to hold the bag.

LEASH WALKING TOOLS FOR SUCCESS!

NOT RECOMMENDED

1. We do NOT recommend attaching the leash to the dog's collar as this can place pressure on the dog's neck and could result in injury.

2. We do NOT recommend the use of retractable leashes for many reasons, including but not limited to the following:

- A consistent length of leash is initially key to training a dog to walk nicely on leash. A retractable leash is, therefore, going to hinder the training process.
- The end of a retractable leash is bulky in the hand.
- Retractable leashes are prone to malfunctioning. The thin cord can snap, injuring the dog, the guardian, or even passersby. The reeling in of the cord can result in burns and cuts. The sudden jerk when a dog runs out of leash can cause soft tissue damage.
- Many dogs are frightened of the sound the leash makes when being reeled in or if the leash handle is dropped.

3. We do NOT generally recommend head halters as they can negatively impact dogs both emotionally and physically. A head halter places pressure on the dog's sensitive muzzle. The jerking of the dog's head can lead to soft tissue damage, and even to damage of the spine. Head halters should only be used if an additional temporary management tool is needed to walk a large dog before skill training has taken place. Trainers should ensure that all pet dog guardians using a head halter are taught the correct way to introduce this tool: The dog should welcome the head halter being put on and not find it aversive! *We advise all pet dog guardians who are considering the use of a head halter to consult their force-free certified dog training professional.

LEASH WALKING TOOLS FOR SUCCESS!

Equipment that Should NEVER be Used

Any equipment that causes psychological or physical pain, harm, or damage. No shock, no prong, no choke and no pain, no fear, no force should ever be employed in the training, behavior modification, care, or management of any pet.

DogNostics Position on Collars

The goal is always to ensure the overall well-being of the animal. Consistent with this it is our position that the use of collars and leads that are intended to apply constriction, pressure, pain, or force around a dog's neck (such as choke chains and prong collars) should be avoided.

Though data demonstrating the exact damage that can be potentially caused by using choke, prong and shock collars is incomplete, soft tissue injuries are common. There are many cases of dogs suffering soft tissue damage, eye problems, strangulation (leading to death), tracheal and/or oesophageal damage, and neurological problems resulting from the use of choke/prong collars.

Evidence indicates that rather than speeding the learning process, harsh training methods slow the training process, add to the animal's stress, and can result in both short-term and long-term psychological damage to animals. As is the case with any harsh training method, damage to the animal-human relationship also occurs.

THE 10 KEY KNOWLEDGE PIECES

KNOWLEDGE 1: WHY DO DOGS PULL?

There are many reasons that dogs pull. Here are some of the main ones:

1. Because the dog has not been taught to walk nicely on a leash.
2. Because they can!
3. Because it works for them.

    Dogs pull to get to other dogs, people, places, smells…

    Pulling gets dogs quicker access to things they want!

    Whenever your dog pulls, taking just one step with them gives a clear signal that pulling works.

    The dog is effectively being reinforced for pulling!

4. Because the dog has been corrected when next to the guardian.

    The dog, therefore, prefers to keep their distance.

    If the guardian jerks or tugs on the leash to teach the dog not to pull, the dog learns that after a loose, slack leash comes pain and discomfort, which is quickly associated with being next to the guardian - To jerk a leash, you first need to slacken it!

5. Because walking on a leash attached to a collar hurts the neck. A tight collar makes it more difficult to breath. Have you ever seen a dog gasping for breath while pulling forwards? They try to escape the discomfort by moving away backward or forward.

6. Because you pull. Your dog is simply pulling back!

7. Because going out for a walk might be the most exciting part of a dog's day. It's, therefore, understandable that they might start pulling on their leash to get where they want to go faster. We recommend that you incorporate lots of different activities throughout the day to provide additional mental and physical enrichment for your dog.

8. Because you walk at a different pace to your dog. It can be hard for a dog to match a human's pace. For example, a larger dog has a longer stride than a smaller dog; more athletic dogs will naturally walk at a quicker pace than more sedentary dogs. Is there a miss-match between you and your dog's pace? If so, rather than asking them to walk at your pace all the time, perhaps you can also sometimes walk at their pace?

THE 10 KEY KNOWLEDGE PIECES

KNOWLEDGE 2: BEHAVIOR AND CONSEQUENCE

1. We need to give dogs feedback, guidance, and encouragement when we are training them and in all our daily interactions with them. Don't wait for a training session to reinforce all those lovely behaviors that you see throughout the day, reinforce them as they occur!

2. Teach your dog what to do, rather than teaching them what not to do!

• You should reward the behaviors that you would like to see more of so that these behaviors are reinforced and will, therefore, increase in frequency, intensity, and duration.

• You shouldn't reward the behaviors that you would prefer your dog not to do; so, for example, we are not going to move forward if our dog is pulling.

3. Punishment should never be frightening or painful.

• When your dog is 'wrong', simply manage your dog and the environment to reduce/eliminate the behaviors that you would like to see less of.

• You can remove rewards. You can remove something from the environment that your dog wants to access, or you can remove your dog from the environment.

KNOWLEDGE 3: THE MECHANICS OF TREAT DELIVERY

1. Where should you keep/hold the treats, prior to delivery?

• We advise the use of a treat bag!

• As you will be doing five repetitions of each training step, you can move five treats into your right hand at the commencement of each set.

• Your right hand will serve as your treat 'dish'.

• You can then take one treat at a time with your left hand to deliver it to your dog.

2. How many treats will you use? A lot! Please make sure that your treat bag is full so that you don't run out!

THE 10 KEY KNOWLEDGE PIECES

3. When, where, and how are treats delivered?

You will mark the correct behavior and feed for position:

• Initially for any sign of a loose leash.

• Then when your dog is in the 'Front' position - opposite, facing, and looking towards you.

• Later, whenever your dog is in the 'Close' position, on your left side. The treats should be delivered using your left hand, straight down your left side. Using your right hand could mean that you inadvertently lure your dog out of position across the front of your body.

• Safely:

• Delivery from a flat hand can be safer than delivering with the treat held between your thumb and fingers.

• Treats should not be thrust into a dog's mouth. Allow your dog to reach forwards an inch or two and take the offered treat. Feeding the treat in this way also offers an element of choice for the dog – Your dog chooses whether they wish to take the treat.

• If your dog is prone to snatching, treats can also be placed on the floor; but feeding from a flat hand, as if you were feeding a pony, should resolve the problem.

• Effectively:

The timing of the reward and the location of your dog when you deliver it, can add extra confirmation to your dog regarding which behavior they are being reinforced for.

An untimely treat that is delivered before or at the same time as the behavior marker or an ill-placed treat that 'pulls' the dog out of position, may not lead to repetition of the desired behavior.

KNOWLEDGE 4: TRAIN-TEST-TRAIN!

To be successful in our training, we need to make sure that we recognize when we should make a small increase in the level of difficulty; when we should continue at the same level; and, when we need to make it easier.

THE 10 KEY KNOWLEDGE PIECES

The Train-Test-Train System is an easy method to follow and allows us to progress at a rate that will lead to success!

The 'Rules of the Game'

1. Count out five treats.
2. Cue the behavior five times.
- Each time your dog responds correctly, mark with a verbal "yes" or a click and deliver a treat.
- Each time your dog responds incorrectly, do not mark, or treat. Set the treat aside as a 'counter'.
3. Repeat until you have no more treats – You have cued (asked for) the behavior five times.
4. Count the number of treats set aside.
- If you have one or no 'counters' set aside, your dog is at least 80% reliable at the current criteria level.

  PUSH - Raise your criteria. Make it slightly more difficult! 
- If you have two counters set aside, your dog is 60% reliable at the current level.

  STICK - Do not raise your criteria yet. Do another set of five and reassess your dog's progress.
- If you have three or more counters set aside, your dog is 40% reliable or less. At this low reinforcement level, dogs may get discouraged and stop playing the training game.

  Temporarily DROP - Lower your criteria. Do a set of five at the easier level and reassess your dog's progress.

Summary:

- 4 or 5 correct responses out of 5 - We can PUSH: Increase the difficulty!
- 3 out of 5 – We need to STICK: Repeat another set of 5 at the current level
- Less than 3 out of 5 – We need to DROP: Make it easier!

THE 10 KEY KNOWLEDGE PIECES

 ## KNOWLEDGE 5: WHAT YOU SHOULD PAY ATTENTION TO

1. A Loose Leash.

We recommend that you hold the leash in your right hand against the front of your body. This will help you maintain a consistent length of leash, which will serve as valuable information for your dog who will learn how far they can move away from you without the leash tightening.

There should not be any tension in the leash. If there is no tension in the leash that means that neither of you are pulling. No gasping dog and no sore arms or wrists for you!

The leash should fall in such a way as to look like a letter J, also sometimes known as having a 'smile' in the leash! One end of the leash hangs from your dog's harness and swoops downward before coming up to the other end, which you are holding in your hand.

2. Your Dog's Position.

Initially, the 'Front' position: Your dog's position opposite and facing you.

Then, the 'Close' position: Your dog's position to your left side. Please note that even if you would like your dog to walk on both sides of you in the future, you should teach one side first. You can then go through the training steps again to teach the other side should you so wish. For those who choose to walk their dog on the right side instead of the left, you can, of course, do so and will simply follow all the training steps with your dog in the 'Side' position: Your dog in position to your right side. Please note, this is not a 'heel' position.

3. Reciprocal Focus

Dog-guardian and guardian-dog! If we expect our dogs to pay attention to us, we should also pay attention to our dogs!

This means no chatting with friends or speaking on the phone. Please give your dog your full attention!

4. High Rate of Reinforcement

THE 10 KEY KNOWLEDGE PIECES

If you are marking and reinforcing your dog's responses at a rate of over 80% you are on the right track! Less than 80% means that your reinforcement rate is too low. This should serve as a clear signal to you that your dog is struggling, and that you need to make the training 'game' a little easier. ***Remember to Train-Test-Train!***

5. Communication of Intention. From you, the guardian, to your dog.

Please always let your dog know what you are about to do. For example, if you are about to set off walking, please communicate this to your dog BEFORE you move: "Let's Go!".

KNOWLEDGE 6: EMPOWER YOUR DOG!

1. Allow your dog to make choices and avoid situations that they are not happy about.

2. Whenever safely possible, allow your dog access to those things they want.

Let your dog choose their own reinforcer.

Simply ask for a nice behavior such as a 'Sit' or the 'Close' or 'Front' position and reinforce the correct response by saying "Go Sniff!", etc.

3. Follow the Leader!

Why not occasionally go for a walk and let your dog take the lead, going wherever they want to? You never know where you might end up and what adventures you might enjoy!

KNOWLEDGE 7: SELF-REINFORCING BEHAVIORS

Some behaviors are self-reinforcing which means that they give the dog intrinsic reward.

1. Pulling on the leash to get to greet someone or arrive at the park quicker or get home quicker or reach the smelly piece of grass…

THE 10 KEY KNOWLEDGE PIECES

The behavior is being repeated because it is being reinforced!

2. When behaviors are trained well and become habitual, they can become self-reinforcing.

Make sure walking on a loose leash is habitual and not pulling!

3. Use a high rate of reinforcement and beat the environment or use 'Grandma's rule' (The Premack Principle).

Make the 'competition' the reinforcer!

Walking nicely results in access to what your dog wants!

KNOWLEDGE 8: ALTERNATIVE REINFORCERS

Throughout the 10 Steps to Walking Nicely on a Loose Leash program, you will use a high-rate of reinforcement and you will use delicious, high-value treats.

1. Please use the same protocol on ALL your walks!

- Whether near your home or out and about in new environments!
- Especially whenever you have a competing environmental factor.

Whether It be a person, dog or even a nice patch of grass!

Whether it be something your dog wants to access or something they want to avoid,

please help your dog to make good decisions by rewarding them!

2. Once the behavior is known, you can introduce a variety of reinforcers.

- You can use different sorts of food, tug toys, balls, squeaky toys, and praise…
- You can also use 'life-rewards' such as, access to play, access to a nice smelly patch of grass, access to a friend!
- You can use anything that your dog loves!

THE 10 KEY KNOWLEDGE PIECES

KNOWLEDGE 9:
DISTRACTIONS – THE ENVIRONMENT THROWS A CURVE BALL!

Does your dog struggle to pass by another dog? Does your dog sometimes pull, bark, or lunge to either get closer to something or to avoid it? Does your dog try to rush towards people or perhaps hide behind you?

Example Situations:
- You notice an off-leash dog.
- A person and/or dog is quickly approaching your 'nervous' dog.
- There is something on the ground that you wish to avoid.

Solutions:
Add distance!
Cue "Let's Go" and remove your dog from these potentially hazardous situations thus avoiding problems, without using force or fearful voice reactions that can contribute to future leash reactivity.

Can't get away? Pay, Pay, Pay! Use the Rapid-Fire Protocol!
The goal here isn't simply to distract your dog. This protocol will not only help your dog to cope better at the current time, but it will also contribute to conditioning a more positive emotional response to the 'trigger' - whatever is proving problematic and triggering your dog's unhappy response.

   1. Begin to feed your dog delicious treats as soon as you see the trigger, preferably before your dog has time to negatively react. Please note that 'low-value' treats will not suffice. The treats need to be something your dog absolutely LOVES!

   2. As the trigger gets nearer, increase the speed of delivery.

   3. When the trigger is very close, begin to rapid-fire the treats: Feed a delicious treat and the second your dog finishes eating it, feed another, and then another. Alternatively, you can

THE 10 KEY KNOWLEDGE PIECES

scatter the treats on the floor. Your dog can use their nose to locate all the delicious treats. Sniffing for the treats can also help your dog relax in what could otherwise be a stressful situation.

    4. As you or the trigger move away, you can slow down the speed at which you are feeding the treats.

    5. When the trigger is out of sight, praise your dog for a job well done!
Please note that this protocol is not contingent on your dog's behavior.

- Your dog does not need to sit, lie down, watch you etc.
- This is not the time to insist on certain behaviors.
- Delivery of the delicious food treats should be continued even if your dog lunges or barks! However, if this occurs your dog will be less likely to eat the food as you are, undoubtedly, too near to the trigger. Please move further away if possible.
- Remember that the goal is to condition a positive emotional response to the trigger (whatever is causing the negative response). It will help if you make this feel like a game!

Static distractions are usually easier to cope with than moving distractions.

TIPS Tip: If your dog is finding it hard to cope with a moving trigger and you cannot increase the distance by moving away, do not walk forwards, employ the rapid-fire protocol while maintaining a stationary position.

IMPORTANT: If you have a problem with leash 'reactivity', please make an appointment with a certified, force-free behaviorist.

KNOWLEDGE 10: MY DOG IS PULLING, WHAT SHOULD I DO?

What should you do if your dog pulls you or lunges forwards?
Firstly, please endeavor to act before this occurs, but if it does…

    1. Don't move forwards, stand firm. Remember that every time you move forwards when your dog is pulling, you are reinforcing the action meaning your dog is more likely to pull in the future. Our goal is to teach your dog that walking next to you with a loose leash means

they get to move forward – and pulling means they don't. The second the lead starts to tighten, stop walking!

   2. Stand still and don't move forward again until the leash is slack.

   3. Communicate with your dog. As soon as the leash slackens, tell your dog "Good boy/-girl", and then walk forward.

   4. Once you are walking forward, increase your rate of reinforcement to keep your dog with you.

   5. Please do NOT build a 'yo-yo' behavior – a dog who pulls and then comes back to you, before pulling forwards again, and then coming back to you again. You can avoid this by praising your dog for coming back to you but only offering a primary reinforcer (a tasty treat) when they are walking at your side (points 3 & 4).

What else can you do?

   6. Use an alert sound – an attention-getting noise – such as a kissy noise, or a jolly "Pup-Pup" to get your dog's attention.

   7. Cue your dog to move into the 'Front' or 'Close' position or lure them into one of these positions.

   8. Cue "This way" or "Let's Go" and change direction.

   9. Try 'stroking' the leash. Make a hand over hand motion as if you are stroking the leash. This will cause a vibration to run down the leash and is often enough to get the dog's attention. Stroking the leash can also help calm your dog.

   10. If necessary, slowly, and gently 'reel' your dog in, shortening the leash using a hand over hand motion.

THE 10 KEY KNOWLEDGE PIECES

This is the rule that dictates that before you can, for example, have some ice-cream, you will need to eat your vegetables; or, before you can watch television, you must do your homework!

So, how can you use 'Grandma's Rule'?

It's simple: Ask for a behavior that you want and reward your dog's nice response with the behavior that your dog wants!

For example,

if your dog is pulling because they want to reach a nice patch of grass or anything else that it would be safe for them to access, you can use what your dog wants as a positive reinforcer for carrying out what you would like your dog to do – You ask for a behavior that you want and then reward the nice response by cueing your dog to carry out the behavior that they want to do.

For example:

1. Your dog pulls forward toward a bush.
2. You ask your dog to come to your side: Cue "Close".
3. Your dog moves into position at your left side.
4. You mark the movement into the 'Close' position by saying, "Yes"
5. You cue "Go sniff" and quickly move forward with your dog to the bush.

GETTING STARTED WITH THE SKILL TRAINING

Our Tips for Success

1. Please initially practice in a quiet, non-distracting environment so that you and your dog can fully concentrate on the training game.

2. Please use a food reward that your dog loves.

3. Once you have successfully achieved all the steps, please go back to the start - Step 1 - and teach again in another non-distracting location!

4. Only when you have successfully gone through all the training steps several times in various non-distracting locations, would you expect your dog to be able to successfully walk nicely in slightly more distracting locations.

5. Remember that 'practice makes perfect' - Practise a lot and reinforce a lot!

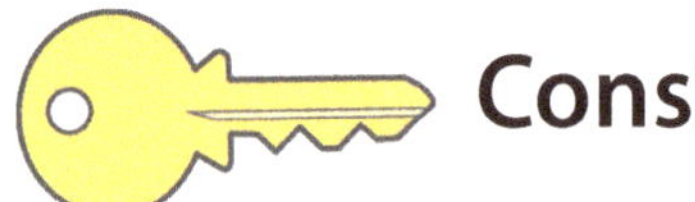 **Consistency is Key!**

Please be consistent with your training each time you go for a walk with your dog!
You should expect walks to take longer while your dog is learning. If you do not have more time, we suggest not walking so far. You may need to stick to shorter walks for a few days. In fact, we encourage you to do lots of leash training in and around your home while you and your dog are learning to walk together.

If you consistently work through the 10 Steps to Walking Nicely on a Loose Leash, and, while out on your walks, strive for and reinforce (reward) all the behaviors that promote walking nicely on a loose leash, your reward will come soon: Enjoyable walks with a happy dog who no longer pulls you along!

Although consistency will lead to a much speedier acquisition of nice leash walking skills and pleasanter walks for both you and your dog, we understand that 'real life' can sometimes get in the way of the very best intentions.

If you're not able to be 100% consistent, for example, you are running late but need to quickly take your dog out, we recommend that you use a different harness to the one that your dog wears while you are working on training nice leash walking skills. Dogs are very clever, and your dog will learn the difference between the two harnesses. They will learn that they can pull

GETTING STARTED WITH THE SKILL TRAINING

while wearing one of the harnesses but not while wearing the other.

Please do note, however, that if you sometimes allow your dog to pull and sometimes don't, it is likely to take your dog longer to learn how to walk nicely on a loose leash.

The Marker Game

"Yes" = "Yes, you did the right thing, orient towards me for a treat!"

Before you begin the training skills, you should effectively condition your verbal marker "yes". The word "yes" is going to let your dog know exactly when they have done the right thing – it marks the correct response. It also serves to let your dog know that a yummy reward is on the way!

Please follow these steps for success:

- Take ten delicious, high-value treats.
- Stand in front of your dog.
- Say a clear "yes" and feed a treat.
- Repeat x 10.

Although in the future, you will use your marker word, "Yes", to communicate to your dog that they did the right thing, when playing the Marker Game, we are simply conditioning a happy emotional response to the word. Therefore, please do not ask for any specific behavior. Your dog can choose to sit, stand, or lie down. It's your dog's choice!

Please play the Marker Game,

- A minimum of three times a day: Once in the morning, once in the afternoon, and once in the evening.
- In all the rooms of your house, followed by your outside areas, for example, in your yard, your garden, on your terrace or deck.

Carrying out the above conditioning should mean that your behavior marker quickly becomes

GETTING STARTED WITH THE SKILL TRAINING

salient. Your dog will pay attention to it and will respond by looking towards you for their treat. Now, when you ask your dog for a particular behavior (that you have taught them to do) and you mark the correct response with your "yes" word, your dog will understand that they have done the right thing and will enthusiastically look to you for praise and a treat! This is going to be crucial for success, not only as you move forward through the 10 Steps to Walking Nicely on a Loose Leash, but also with ANY skill that you train!

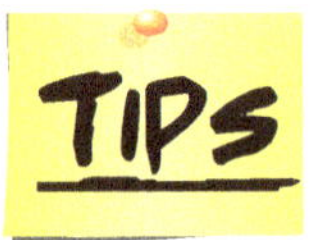 **_A Quick Tip:_**

Once conditioned, your verbal "yes" marker can also be useful when out and about if your dog is slightly unsure about something. Let's imagine that your dog looks towards something or someone that could perhaps trigger a fearful or anxious response from your dog (e.g., a strange person, object, or unknown dog); you 'mark' the perceiving (looking towards whatever it is) by saying "yes"; on hearing the "Yes", your dog orients towards you; you feed a tasty treat and then give your dog another cue e.g., "Let's Go"!

 **_Please note:_**

   • You can use a clicker to mark a behavior instead of a verbal "yes"! If you are going to use a clicker in the future, we highly recommend that after you have played the Marker Game using a verbal "yes", you play it again using your clicker!

   • A verbal marker or a clicker isn't going to work if your dog is hearing impaired. Choose a visual marker instead. A hand-flash (a quick opening and closing of your hand) can be a good option.

   • If your dog is both hearing & visually impaired, a light two-finger tap on your dog's side can be a good option! You will also need to make sure that the food you use is nice and 'smelly', as this will make it easier for your dog to locate.

PREREQUISITE SKILLS

Before beginning the 10 Steps to Walking Nicely on a Loose Leash, we recommend that you work through the following three training games: Stand on Leash, Front, and Close. Please read the information below to learn how to teach these prerequisite skills!

'Stand' on Leash

Goal: Teach your dog how to be on a leash with no pulling, straining, or lunging. You can be stationary or move a few steps in either direction. You will use the full scope of the 2m (6ft) leash without any tension in the leash.

For this exercise, there is no need to work in sets of five. You should have at least 20 delicious treats ready to deliver!

Please follow these steps for success:

   1. Quickly mark and reinforce anything that your dog does other than putting tension on the leash – Say a verbal "yes" or click and follow up with a tasty treat.
   2. You will 'rapid-fire' mark and reward all correct responses.
   3. You will not mark and reward if there is any tension on the leash. Simply stand firm and the second the tension is released say "yes" and reinforce!
We want to ensure maximum feedback. This is a conversation between you, the guardian, and your dog.

Please make sure to use treats that your dog loves and begin in a non-distracting environment.

The 'Front' Position

Goal: Your dog sits or stands directly in front of and facing you. This does not need to be a precision behavior; we simply want your dog opposite you and looking in your direction.

Criterion 1 – Lure Your Dog into Position

1. With your dog standing on a loose leash, take a treat between your thumb and two fingers. This should look like a bird's beak holding food.

2. Present the treat a couple of inches in front of your dog's nose.

3. Lure your dog into the 'Front' position – opposite and facing you. You will do this by keeping your hand in front of your dog's nose but slowly moving it into position near to or against the front of your body. Please make sure the speed of the movement is neither too quick nor too slow so that your dog can easily follow the treat!

4. Say "yes" or click as your dog comes into the 'Front' position.

5. Open your hand flat – 'Pony' hand – and feed the delicious treat. The opening of your hand not only signals to your dog that they can take the treat, but it also serves as an additional behavior marker letting your dog know that they have done the right thing.

6. Repeat five times.

> Remember to Train-Test-Train!
> 5/5 -> Push – Move to criterion 2
> 3 or 4/5 -> Stick – Repeat this criterion
> 1 or 2/5 -> Drop – Lower the criteria (Make the game easier)

Here are some suggestions regarding how you can make the game easier:

- Increase the 'value' of the treat.
- Move to a quieter location.
- Repeat the Stand on Leash game and, after marking any behavior that is consistent with a loose leash, offer the reward directly in front of your body – Your dog should naturally focus on you and move into the 'Front' position to collect their reward!
- Step into position yourself – In this case, your dog does not need to do anything; you

PREREQUISITE SKILLS

imply step into position and mark and reward!

Criterion 2 – Fade the Treat

We do not want your dog to become dependent on you having food in your hand, so we need to 'fade' the treat. With your dog standing on a loose leash, you are going to lure your dog into position opposite and facing you, but this time you will have no food in your hand. Your hand motion will become a visual cue (a hand signal) that communicates to your dog that you would like them to follow. Your dog will begin to understand that the food does not need to be in your hand, they will still receive the reinforcement!

1. Present your 'bird's beak' a couple of inches in front of your dog's nose. You are no longer holding a treat but presenting your hand in the same way will help your dog realize that they should follow.
2. Lure your dog into the 'Front' position – opposite and facing you.
3. Say "yes" or click as your dog comes into the 'Front' position and open your hand flat.
4. Quickly feed a delicious treat.
5. Repeat five times.

If your dog does not follow your empty hand, you can temporarily reintroduce the treat and then fade it more gradually:
 • Try twice with a treat, followed by once without, followed by two more with.
 • You can then try once with, followed by once without, once with, once without, once with.
 • Then, twice without, once with, twice without.
 • Until your dog successfully follows your empty 'bird's beak'.

Now generalize the behavior:
 • Repeat Criterion 2 facing different directions (North, South, East, and West).
 • Repeat in different locations.

Name the behavior:
 • Once your dog can reliably move into position, you can introduce a verbal cue.
 • We use the cue "Front", but you can choose any word that you want.
 • Consistently use the same word – your chosen cue - just as or before your dog moves into position and they will soon learn what it means.

PREREQUISITE SKILLS

The 'Close' Position

Goal: Your dog moves into position, sitting or standing on your left side. Your dog should be near to and parallel to your left leg. Your dog's shoulders should be in line with your leg.

• You can lure your dog into the 'Close' position or, if you need to make the game easier, you can simply step into position yourself so that you are standing next to and on the right-hand side of your dog.

• Say "yes" or click as your dog comes into the 'Close' position.

• Reward each successful response with a tasty treat. This will reinforce the behavior!

• After a successful set of five repetitions, please fade your food lure.

• You can proof the behavior by practicing bringing your dog into the 'Close' position from different angles.

• Once your dog can reliably move into position, you can introduce a verbal cue. We use the cue "Close", but you can choose any word that you want. Just consistently use the same word just as or before your dog moves into position and they will soon learn what it means.

THE 10 STEPS TO WALKING NICELY ON LEASH

If you have worked through the previous training games, you and your dog have already made a fabulous start on the road to success! It's now time to work through the 10 Steps to Walking Nicely on a Loose Leash!

STEP 1 – FOLLOW ME FOR ONE STEP!

GOAL Goal: Your dog will follow you for one step as you walk backward.

Use a HIGH-VALUE food reward!

1. Stand in front of your dog - Your dog is in the 'Front' position: Directly in front of and facing you. If taught, you can cue your dog to come into position. Alternatively, you can simply step into this position, or you can lure your dog into position with a tasty treat.
2. Make sure your dog is ready. You only begin when you have your dog's focus on you!
3. Take one step backward. We advise that your step be the approximate length of your dog.
4. Mark the behavior of following you with a verbal 'yes' word or a click.
5. Reinforce to mouth just in front of your legs - You and the dog are facing each other.
6. Repeat x 5.

Train-Test-Train!
- 4 or 5 out of 5 correct responses? You can progress to Step 2!

If your dog does not follow you, do not progress to Step 2!

- 3 correct responses? We advise that you repeat this Step.
- Less than 3 correct responses? Make the game easier!

How can you make the game easier?
Lure your dog!

1. Stand facing our dog.

THE 10 STEPS TO WALKING NICELY ON LEASH

2. Hold a yummy treat between your thumb, index finger, and middle finger - Your hand should look like a bird's beak holding food.

3. Present the treat just in front of your dog's nose.

4. Lure your dog forward as you take one step backward. We advise that your step be the approximate length of your dog.

5. Mark the correct response (following you) with a verbal 'yes' word or a click.

6. Reinforce by delivering the treat to your dog's mouth just in front of your legs. Please open your hand flat to deliver the treat, as if you were feeding a pony!

7. Repeat x 5.

Train-Test-Train!

• 4 or 5 out of 5 correct responses? You can progress to Step 1! Or, if necessary, repeat the luring motion x 5 without food in your hand.

 If your dog does not follow you, do not progress to Step 1!

• 3 correct responses? We advise that you repeat this Step
• Less than 3 correct responses? Make the game easier!

How can you make the game easier?
Increase the amount of food in your hand!

1. Stand facing your dog.

2. Take a whole bunch of smelly treats in your hand.

3. Close your fingers loosely over the treats so that you don't drop them, but so that your dog can clearly see and smell them.

4. Present your hand full of treats just in front of your dog's nose.

5. Take one step backward while luring your dog to follow you.

6. Mark the dog's movement, following you.

7. Reinforce by feeding your dog several of the treats in your hand.

8. Repeat x 5.

THE 10 STEPS TO WALKING NICELY ON LEASH

More suggestions to make Step 1 easier.

- Step back by just half a dog length.
- Increase the value of your treat.
- Make sure you are using treats that your dog LOVES!
- Increase YOUR enthusiasm for the game: Excitement is contagious! Make happy sounds to encourage your dog to follow you and add a little bounce into your step!
- Move to a less distracting location.
- Play the game at a different time of the day when your dog is feeling a little more energetic.

Why step backward instead of simply walking forward?

- It is easier to follow someone when we can see their face as we have mutual focus and a connection with each other.
- It is more difficult to follow someone who simply moves away with their back to us as the connection is lost.

 Additional Tips for Success

1. Be enthusiastic about the game! If you are lacking enthusiasm, your dog is likely to lack it too!

2. Make sure that your steps are appropriate for your dog. Each of your steps should be roughly equivalent to the length of your dog.

3. If your dog is struggling to follow you, try making the same motion that you made when you were holding a treat – Make your hand look like a bird's beak when you are luring, then clearly open your hand as you say "yes" or click, and quickly deliver the reinforcer. Your dog will begin to understand that the food does not need to be in your hand, he/she will still receive the reinforcement!

4. If your dog is still struggling, the treat can be temporarily reintroduced. Try one repetition with a treat, and then one without, followed by one with, and two without. Until finally, the treat is no longer needed as your dog will follow you for five steps without a treat in your hand.

THE 10 STEPS TO WALKING NICELY ON LEASH

STEP 2 – FOLLOW ME FOR FIVE STEPS!

Goal: Dog on a leash follows you, with enthusiasm and with no hesitation, as you walk backward for up to 5 steps.

1. Stand in front of your dog - Your dog is in the 'Front' position: Directly in front of and facing you. You can simply step into this position, or you can lure your dog into position with a tasty treat.
2. Make sure your dog is ready. You only begin when you have your dog's focus on you!
3. Take two steps backward. We advise that each of your steps be the approximate length of your dog.
4. Mark the behavior of following you with a verbal 'yes' word or a click.
5. Reinforce to mouth just in front of your legs - You and the dog are facing each other.
6. Repeat x 5.

Please do:

1. One set of two steps (five repetitions)
2. One set of three steps
3. One set of four steps
4. One set of five steps

Remember to Train-Test-Train!
- 4 or 5 out of 5 correct responses? Increase by one step!
- 3 correct responses? Repeat the current number of steps!
- Less than 3 correct responses? Make the game easier! Reduce the number of steps!

Move to Step 3 if you have a push! (Five out of five correct responses – your dog following you on a loose leash as you walk backward for five steps). 👆

THE 10 STEPS TO WALKING NICELY ON LEASH

STEP 3 – STEP BACK & THEN TURN FORWARD!

Goal: Dog follows you on a loose leash as you step backward. You then turn to face the same direction as your dog!

1. Stand in front of your dog - Your dog is in the 'Front' position.
2. Make sure your dog is ready.
3. Step back with your right leg, away from your dog.
4. Turn 180-degree so that you are facing the same direction as your dog - You can do this by pivoting on your right foot.
5. Bring your left leg forward one step - so that you bring your feet in line with each other.
6. Mark and reinforce in the 'Close' position - Your dog's head should be at the side of your left leg.
7. Repeat x 5.

Train-Test-Train!
- Move to the next criterion if you have a push! (Five correct responses) 
- 3 or 4 correct responses? Stick! (Repeat Step 3). 
- 1 or 2 correct responses? Drop! (Make the exercise easier. Go back to Step 2).

TIPS   Tips for Success
- Practice the 180-degree without your dog before beginning with your dog!
- Hold your leash in your right hand or work 'hands-free' (attach your leash to your belt or wear it across your body).
- This leaves your left hand free!
- Use your left hand to deliver the treat straight down the side of your left leg. This will help keep your dog straight. If you use the opposite hand, you might 'pull' your dog out of position when you reward.
- If for any reason you are walking your dog on the right instead of the left, you would hold your leash in your left hand, leaving your right hand free to reward straight down your right side!

STEP 4 – STEP BACK & WALK FORWARD FIVE STEPS

Goal: Dog follows you on a loose leash as you step backward and then turn and walk forward for up to five steps.

1. Begin with your dog in the 'Front' position
2. Step back with your right leg, away from your dog.
3. Turn 180-degree so that you are facing the same direction as your dog.
4. Take one step forward.
5. Mark and reinforce in the 'Close' position. Your dog's head should be at the side of your left leg.
6. Repeat x 5, systematically increasing the number of steps until you are walking forward for five steps with your dog at your left side!

Train-Test-Train!

• Move to the next criterion if you have a push! (Five correct responses) – Add an additional step forward.

• 3 or 4 correct responses? Stick! - Repeat the same number of steps forward.

• 1 or 2 correct responses? Drop! (Make the exercise easier). Reduce the number of steps forward.

If we follow the above criteria, we will mark and reinforce after one step forward; after two steps forward; after three steps forward; after four steps forward, and after five steps forward. Wow, our dog was being reinforced for one step but now needs to do five steps before earning their reward! That may be too difficult for some dogs. If your dog is finding this too difficult, you can make the exercise easier by thinning the reinforcement (the number of steps required, per reward gained) more gradually.

THE 10 STEPS TO WALKING NICELY ON LEASH

For example,

- Mark and reinforce each individual step for five steps – one step-mark-reinforce, one more step-mark-reinforce; one more step step-mark-reinforce, etc.
- Now, mark and reinforce for two steps x 5 (more difficult)
- Then, mark and reinforce for three steps x 5 (more difficult)
- Now, mark and reinforce for just one step again x 5 (easier)
- Then, mark and reinforce for four steps x 5 (more difficult)

The key here is that although we are gradually increasing the number of steps, we sometimes make it easier. Even when your dog is succeeding, it does not always get more difficult!

THE 10 STEPS TO WALKING NICELY ON LEASH

STEP 5 – TEN INDIVIDUAL STEPS FORWARD!

Goal: Dog walks near your left side, on a loose leash, as you walk forward for ten steps, reinforcing EVERY step!

1. Begin with your dog in the 'Close' position – Your dog is standing parallel and close to your left leg.
2. Make sure your dog is ready.
3. Walk forward one step, mark & reinforce in the 'Close' position – Your dog's head should be at the side of your left leg.
4. Walk forward one more step, mark & reinforce.
5. Walk forward one more step, mark & reinforce.
6. You will mark and reinforce each step forward for ten steps!

Remember to Train-Test-Train! You will only move to Step 6 if your dog is successful at Step 5!

THE 10 STEPS TO WALKING NICELY ON LEASH

STEP 6 – WALK TOGETHER FOR TEN STEPS!

Goal: Dog walks near your left side, on a loose leash, as you walk forward for ten steps. Reinforcement is systematically thinned with the aim of rewarding after ten steps!

1. Begin with your dog in the 'Close' position.
2. Make sure your dog is ready.
3. Walk forward one step, mark & reinforce in the 'Close' position.
4. Systematically increase the number of steps that you walk forward up to ten steps:
- 2 steps, mark and reinforce
- 3 steps, mark and reinforce
- 4 steps, mark and reinforce
- 5 steps, mark and reinforce
- 6 steps, mark and reinforce
- 7 steps, mark and reinforce
- 8 steps, mark and reinforce
- 9 steps, mark and reinforce
- 10 steps, mark and reinforce

STEP 7 – WALK TOGETHER FOR TWENTY STEPS!

GOAL Goal: Dog walks near your left side, on a loose leash, as you walk forward for twenty steps.

A variable ratio schedule of reinforcement is used to help make this achievable for your dog.

1. Begin with your dog in the 'Close' position.
2. Make sure your dog is ready.
3. Walk forward ten steps, mark & reinforce in the 'Close' position.
4. Use a variable ratio schedule of reinforcement to build from 10 to 20 steps. We suggest working around an average of 10.

For example,
- 11 steps, mark and reinforce
- 5 steps, mark and reinforce
- 12 steps, mark and reinforce
- 9 steps, mark and reinforce
- 13 steps, mark and reinforce

$11 + 5 + 12 + 9 + 13 = 50 \div 5 = 10$ (The average number of steps that gains reinforcement).

Now take a break and then continue. You may be able to continue in the same session or perhaps you will continue later in the day. Listen to your dog! If your dog is tired, please do not continue, come back to this later in the day!

Continue to increase the number of steps using your variable ratio of reinforcement.
For example,

- 14 steps, mark and reinforce
- 2 steps, mark and reinforce
- 15 steps, mark and reinforce
- 3 steps, mark and reinforce

THE 10 STEPS TO WALKING NICELY ON LEASH

• 16 steps, mark and reinforce

$14 + 2 + 15 + 3 + 16 = 50 \div 5 = 10$

Take another break!

Continue to increase the number of steps using your variable ratio of reinforcement.
For example,

• 4 steps, mark and reinforce
• 17 steps, mark and reinforce
• 8 steps, mark and reinforce
• 18 steps, mark and reinforce
• 3 steps, mark and reinforce

$4 + 17 + 8 + 3 + 18 = 50 \div 5 = 10$

Take another break!

Continue to increase the number of steps using your variable ratio of reinforcement.
For example,

• 4 steps, mark and reinforce
• 19 steps, mark and reinforce
• 2 steps, mark and reinforce
• 5 steps, mark and reinforce
• 20 steps, mark and reinforce

$4 + 19 + 2 + 5 + 20 = 50 \div 5 = 10$

Congratulations, you have accomplished twenty steps!

THE 10 STEPS TO WALKING NICELY ON LEASH

STEP 8 – LET'S CHANGE DIRECTION: "THIS WAY!"

GOAL Goal: Introduce changes in direction to the left and right by walking backward to prompt your dog to follow.

1. Begin with your dog in the 'Close' position.
2. Make sure your dog is ready.
3. Walk forward with your dog.
- Cue "This Way" and walk backward making a 90-degree turn left or right.
- Exaggerate your body language to make your change of direction as clear as possible. Dogs are very good at reading body language signals.
4. Mark the turn.
5. Reinforce with your dog in the 'front' position.
6. You should then make a 180-degree turn so that you are facing the same direction as the dog, and repeat the above x 5

Please note your dog does not yet understand the cue "This Way"

- Usually, we do not introduce new cues until the behavior is fluent (reliable and strong).
- If you are in any doubt as to whether your dog will follow you, please do not say the cue. However, as you will initially walk backward to change direction and exaggerate your body language, your dog, who you are focusing on and who is focusing on you because they are enjoying the game, should follow!
- With repetition of the words "This Way", your dog will learn that this cue means you are about to turn but be in no doubt, he will still be watching your body language!

THE 10 STEPS TO WALKING NICELY ON LEASH

STEP 9 – HOW TO MAKE A U-TURN!

Goal: Introduce U-turns, so that you can quickly walk in the opposite direction, by walking backward to prompt your dog to follow.

1. Begin with your dog in the 'Close' position.
2. Make sure your dog is ready.
3. Walk forward with your dog.
4. Cue "Let's Go" and walk backward in such a way as to prompt your dog to make a 180-degree turn, so that your dog is now going in the opposite direction.
5. Mark the turn.
6. You, the guardian, should then make a 180-degree turn (pivot) so that you are facing the same direction as your dog.
7. Reinforce with your dog in the 'Close' position (at the side of your left leg).
8. Repeat x 5.

Once you have introduced your "Let's Go" cue, we encourage you to use it whenever you are about to set off walking with your dog or change direction. The cue communicates to your dog that they should move with you!

THE 10 STEPS TO WALKING NICELY ON LEASH

STEP 10 – LET'S STOP TOGETHER!

 Goal: Offer reinforcement for stopping when you stop!

1. Begin with your dog in the 'Close' position.
2. Make sure your dog is ready.
3. Cue "Let's Go" and set off walking with your dog.
4. Stop (No verbal cue).
5. Mark as soon as your dog stops.
6. Reinforce with your dog in the 'Close' position.
7. Repeat x 5.

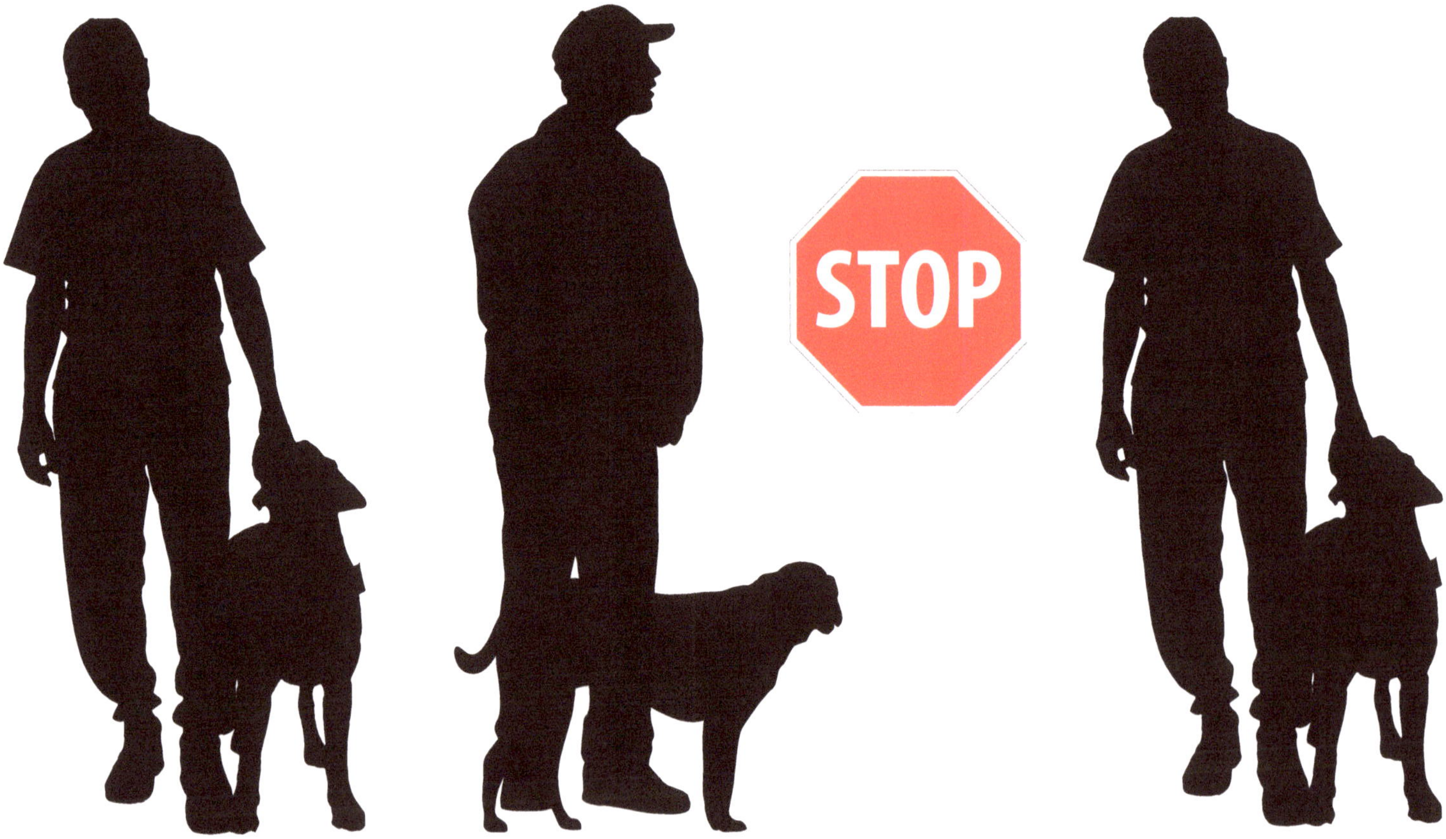

PROOF & MAINTAIN YOUR NEW LEASH WALKING SKILLS

Now that you have taught your dog to walk nicely on a loose leash, you need to proof the skill so that your dog can reliably walk nicely in lots of different circumstances. You also need to maintain the skill. If you don't practice a new skill, old habits can soon re-emerge.

TIPS Here are some tips for you:

- Practice your newly acquired leash walking skills in lots of new environments.
- We advise you to systematically work your way through the 10 Steps to Walking Nicely on a Loose Leash in lots of different locations.
- Remember to begin in the least distracting environment and gradually build up to more challenging ones.
- When moving to more challenging environments, initially increase your rate of reinforcement.
- Gradually introduce more distractions. This can include people, toys on the floor, other dogs, different noises, different environments, for example, the town, the countryside, the seafront promenade/boardwalk… Tip: start with small distractions.
- Practice changing pace. We love the cues "Quick-Quick" and "S-L-O-W"!
- For dogs that are happy around other dogs, it can also be lots of fun and good practice to walk with friends!

TWO FUN GAMES

There are many games that you can play to build on your leash walk skills and provide additional mental and physical enrichment for your dog, as well as being lots of fun for you both!

In this section, we have included two games that we think you will enjoy: The Wobbles and The Chatterbox!

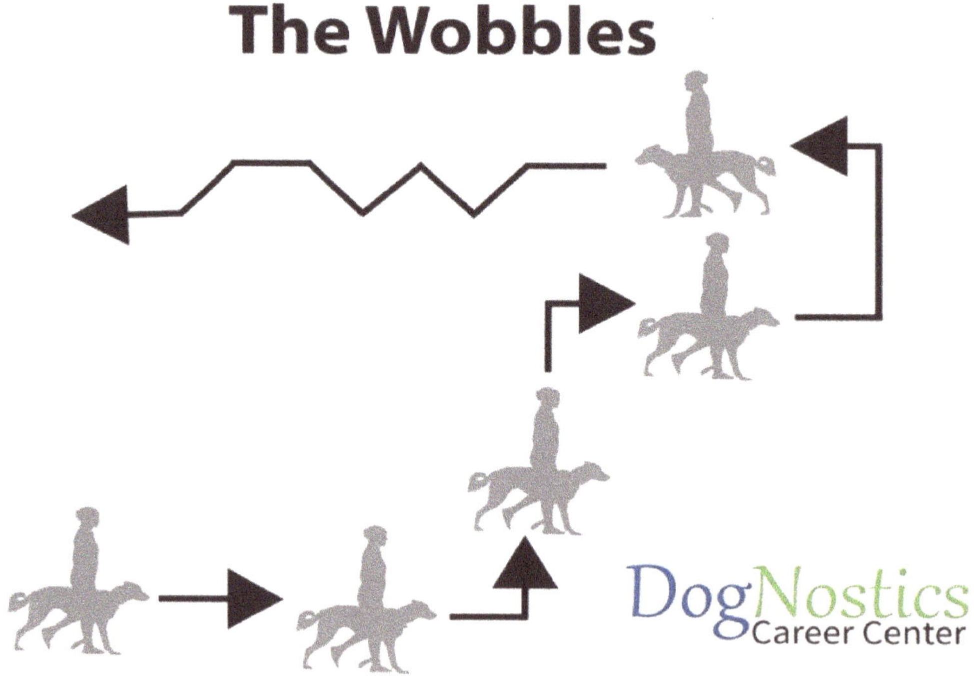

This unpredictable game helps promote focus on you; discourages pulling as your dog never knows which direction they will be moving in next; and encourages communication of intention from you to your dog.

The Wobbles can also be a useful strategy to use if you have a dog who tends to pull one way on their walk. Depending on your dog, this might occur on the outwards stretch of the journey or once you begin to head for home. Simply play The Wobbles game on that stretch of the journey!

You can also play The Wobbles game at any time you think your dog is heading towards the end of the leash.

TWO FUN GAMES

How to play:

  • Cue your dog to walk forward: "Let's Go!". If needed, you can initially walk backward to help gain your dog's attention.

  • Incorporate the following movements and direction changes into the game:
    • Go Straight
    • Cue "This Way" and turn left (90° anticlockwise)
    • Cue "This Way" and turn right (90° clockwise)
    • Cue "Let's Go" and turn 180° and walk back in the opposite direction
    • Walk in a zigzag
    • Walk in a 360° circle
  • Remember to mark and reinforce all correct responses!

The movements appear very random but must be cued. Please remember to communicate your intention.

The Wobbles

TWO FUN GAMES

The Chatterbox

In this focus encouraging game, we make use of three different reinforcers!

    1. The first reinforcer (reward) is the functional reinforcer. What is reinforcing your dog when they pull? Movement!

    2. The second reinforcer is social interaction – Attention in the form of eye contact and enthusiastic chatter!

    3. The third reinforcer is something all dogs (and people) love – Delicious food treats!

It's a good idea to play this game with two humans first. We hope that you have a friend or family member who can play with you! One person will be the 'handler' and one will initially play the role of the dog! This allows you both to practice the mechanics of moving your feet and stopping your feet, as well as providing feedback via all the reinforcement consequences!

How to play:

  • The dog (initially another human) is oriented towards you, the handler. You will both be standing opposite and facing each other, holding opposite ends of the loose leash.

  • While 'the dog' is focused on the handler, looking in your direction, you, the handler, move backward and the person playing the role of the dog follows you. Remember, movement is the first reward!

  • Praise your dog as he/she follows by chattering enthusiastically! Praise is the second reward.

  • Deliver a food reinforcer. The third reward - Make sure it is something the recipient loves

The Chatterbox

TWO FUN GAMES

and is willing to work for!

What if the 'dog' doesn't follow?

• If the dog (in this case your family member or friend) loses focus, is distracted, looks away or stops following, you, the handler, should stop. No movement and no words. You simply wait.

• As soon as 'the dog' looks back towards you, the game begins again – You begin to move and praise.

Switch Roles!

You will play the role of the dog and your friend/family member will be the handler. Swapping roles helps you understand how your dog feels on the end of the leash.

Increase the Level of Difficulty.

A further challenge can be introduced by beginning to walk forwards.

You can also play the game in lots of different locations. We are sure you will brighten anyone's day who happens to pass by!

Now Play the Game with Your Dog!

This game should be lots of fun but requires 100% focus of the handler on the dog and constant chatter – 'Good girl, good dog, excellent job, well done, you're so good!'. The words used aren't important but the enthusiasm with which they are delivered is paramount!

The Chatterbox

CONCLUSION

We wish you every success with your leash walking skills and hope that you have lots of fun working through the 10 Steps to Walking Nicely on a Loose Leash!

Please remember that for maximum success, you should:

- Continue to practice.
- Practice in less distracting environments before practicing in more distracting environments.
- Practice all the components together while you are walking your dog.
- Initially endeavor to walk in less distracting environments, where there are not lots of people and not lots of other dogs.
- The aim is for your dog to be successful, so please do not introduce challenges that they are not yet able to overcome!
- The environment itself is distracting enough with lots of sights, sounds, and smells. You do not need the added difficulty are passers-by!
- You have taught all these wonderful behaviors so all there is left to do is generalize them to different environments; proof them with lots of practice; maintain them with lots of positive reinforcement!

Notes